Expert Enough

The Fastest Way to Create a Career as a Go-To Authority

Russell Davis

I0475505

Table of Contents

Introduction

Congratulations on purchasing your personal copy of *Expert Enough.* Thank you for doing so.

The following chapters will discuss some of the many ways that you can become an expert in your chosen field.

You will discover how important it is to find your particular niche before you try to become an expert in a field. It's better to love what you're doing, rather than do it because it will make you money.

The final chapter will explore how you can continue to grow your knowledge in your field so that you will always remain an expert.

There are plenty of books on this subject on the market, thanks again for choosing this one! Every effort was made to ensure it is full of as much useful information as possible. Please enjoy!

Congratulations on downloading your personal copy of *Expert Enough.* Thank you for doing so.

Find Your Niche

Figuring out your niche is the biggest part of becoming an expert. If you don't have something to become an expert in; then you can't become an expert. A niche, if you don't already know, is a place or a position that you feel comfortable in and are suited for. There are many ways that you can find your niche, and I'm going to cover two.

5-Steps

You're looking to become an expert in a field, and subsequently, in business, but you find that you're being held back because you can't find your niche. This can be extremely tricky. You may have already spent time writing a list of everything you're passionate about and interested in, yet you don't feel any closer to finding the right area.

Putting all that pressure on yourself to figure out your niche can cause brain paralysis. It's important to find that right niche, but sometimes it's better just to get started. When you get started, you can start to test out your different ideas. This way you are able to learn from failed business attempts and pick a new niche, or a new way to go about your career.

Here are five steps to help you figure out your niche:

1. Find what you are passionate about and are interested in.

Chances are you have already done this; if not, write a list of 10 areas that you are passionate about. At some point, business is going to push you. If you are in a business that you care nothing about, your chances of quitting are higher.

That doesn't mean you must find that perfect business. If you can make sure that you love some part of the job, you will be more likely to stay with it. If there is nothing about it that you like, then you probably won't stay with it.

If you seem to be having a problem figuring out what you like, here are some questions to get your headed in the right direction:

- What do you like to do with your free time? What are the things that you look forward to when there is nothing else going on?

- What are the magazines that you like to read? What are the topics that you love learning about the most?

- Are there any organizations you are a part of?

2. Figure out the problems that you are capable of solving.

Now that you have your list of 10, you can start to narrow down your choices. To become an expert and create a business that will last, you have to figure out the target customers and their problems. Then you need to find out if you can solve their problems. Here are some methods that you could use to identify problems that a niche may have:

- Talk to your target group one-on-one. Come up with a way to ask the right questions so that you can get the best answers.

- Look through forums. Look at forums that are specific to your niche, and pay attention to what is being discussed. What are the questions being asked? What are their problems?

- Look through keywords. Look at keyword combinations on sites like Google AdWords or Trends. This will show you some popular search phrases that can help you.

3. Look at the competition.

Competition shouldn't be considered as a bad thing. This could be seen as a sign that you have found a good niche. Make sure that you thoroughly look at their sites. Make a spreadsheet and log the different locations that you find based on your niche.

Then look to see if there is a way that you can stand out from your competitors. Can you still rank with searches? Can you create something that is unique? This is what to look for to find a niche that you can easily slide into:

- Content that's low-quality. It'll be easy to beat out competition if your competition isn't creating high-quality content.

- Little transparency. If your competition is mainly corporate, and you choose to put a face with your service, you're going to stand out against your faceless competitors.

- Very little paid competition. If the keywords that you found returns a lot of search volume, but you don't see a lot of paid advertising and competition, you have a good opportunity to stand-out.

4. Figure out how profitable your niche is.

You should be pretty close to figuring out what your niche is going to be. You may not have things narrowed down to one single idea, but you should have a couple that you like. Now you can look at the amount of money that you could possibly make within your niche. ClickBank is a good place to begin looking.

Begin to look at top services within your niche. If your search doesn't turn up anything, that's a bad sign. This could mean that people haven't been able to monetize that particular niche.

If you find a decent amount of services, but not too many, that's a good sign. Write down the different price points so that you can get an idea of how you should price your products.

There's also no need come up with your own product. You can choose to partner with site owners, advertisers, or creators in your niche and earn commission while you are also working on your ideas.

5. Test what you have thought of.

You now have plenty of information to help you choose your niche, and the only thing that you have to do now is testing it. A simple way to test your idea is to create a landing page for pre-sales. Then drive traffic there with some advertising.

If you don't receive any pre-sales, don't get discouraged. You could still have picked a viable niche. This could just mean that you haven't picked the right service, or you didn't sell it right.

60-Minutes

We've already looked at one way to figure out your niche, but that might not have been a good way for you. Each person is different, so here's another way to figure out a niche.

1. Write down everything that you are skilled or talented at.

Be completely honest with this one because these answers go through to the following questions. Know the difference between things that you are good at versus things that you wish you were good at. Is becoming proficient at something that you have always wanted to learn feasible, or is it just a pipe dream? Set aside any judgment and focus solely on your talents, and not whether those talents will make you money.

2. Out of those talents, which ones do you enjoy doing?

Your brain and heart need to be in agreement; otherwise, you'll be in disequilibrium. When you are in this state, things will feel right with your heart, but your brain will disagree with everything, and vice versa.

Take your first list, and order them with what you like to do the most, and what you like to do the least. Then ask yourself what eliminations you can make.

3. Out of the things that you enjoy doing, are there any that people need?

If there is one that stands out the most, congratulations, you now have an audience of one. A little research will help you to narrow down your choices. Look at demographics on websites that offer them, so that you can get an idea if you should pursue a niche, or how to seek a niche.

4. Of the needs that you have figured out, which ones will people pay for?

Pay is the keyword. Your parents may be willing to give you a few dollars for something you make, but that's not going to help you in the long run. If there is one person out there that will pay for your product, then chances are there are others that will too.

Make sure you're completely honest. You may love playing a game of football with friends, but if you've got a 145-pound frame, you're going to be in for an uphill battle.

These four questions shouldn't take any longer than an hour to do if you actually know yourself. If you don't, then you may find that it takes you longer, and that's okay as well. It's important to take the time now, so you don't waste time down the road.

Improve Your Knowledge

Now that you have figured out your niche, it's time to start learning more about it. If you followed the above questions, then should have picked something that you already know a lot about. Even though you may think that you know all there is to know about your niche, you probably don't. Things are changing all the time, and it's important to know as much as possible.

This doesn't mean that you have to go to school and pay tuition. This can simply mean researching your niche online, reading books, and taking online courses. There are also some general ways to increase your general knowledge that will help you learn things faster.

General Intelligence

The brain has to be exercised like all the other muscles in your body. If you work your brain as often as you can, and in the right ways, you will become a better learner, thinker, and more focused. If you choose not to use your brain and harm it with harmful things, then your ability to learn and think will start to deteriorate.

These are five ways that you can increase your brain's strength and productivity:

1. Minimize your TV intake.

This is hard for people to do. It's most people's favorite pastime to sit in front of the television and veg out. The problem with TV is it doesn't allow your brain to work or to recharge. Don't you find yourself feeling drained after you have watched TV for a few hours straight? Eyes are red, sore, and dry from focusing on the screen.

When you want to relax, read a book. Maybe you don't like to read, instead, listen to music. When you spend time with people, choose to talk to them instead of watching TV. These things will work your mind more than watching television.

2. Work Out

You may think that if you chose to read a book instead of working out that you would learn more. Not necessarily. The time you spend working out will lead to better learning because you will have better productivity afterward. Working out will help you to clear your head and gives you energy. You will feel invigorated and will be able to concentrate more.

3. Read challenging books.

Most people enjoy reading popular books like suspense fiction, but they don't typically stimulate your mind. To help improve your writing and thinking read books that you have to focus on. A classic novel is a good choice because it will change the way you look at the world. It's ok if you have to look up some words, and don't fear the dense reading. Re-read things if you need to and take your time when reading and you'll get used to the way the author writes.

4. Get plenty of sleep

Sleep deprivation is only going to make concentration even harder. If you go to bed at a decent hour and get eight hours of sleep, you will feel more rejuvenated. If you stay up late and try to compensate by sleeping in, you're going to be lethargic and unable to focus. If you make a point of getting up earlier, you will give yourself more productive hours, and you will have better mental acuity.

If you are presented with a chance to do so, take a short nap during the day, no more than 20 minutes. This would help you to beat a wave of drowsiness if it were to hit you. If your nap lasts longer than 20 minutes, you will likely wake up lethargic.

5. Reflect

Life can become hectic, and you probably won't even realize it. You'll find it harder to concentrate because of your thoughts. Make sure you have some alone time to reflect and organize your thoughts and line up your responsibilities. After your reflection, you will understand the things that are the most important. Any unimportant things won't bother you.

These tips may not seem like much, but they will help you to be able to learn and focus better so that you can take in as much information as possible. Now that you know some general tips that will help you learn let's look at some ways to learn information about your niche.

Learning

With the internet, you have a lot of information at your fingertips. Most of that information can be used and found at no cost. This means you don't have a reason not to be able to learn as much as you want and need about your niche.

Read:

The easiest thing you can do is read about your niche. This could be articles online or books. Start doing some research and find some books, articles, and websites that are based on your niche.

Find Books:

Look for books based on your niche. Find ones that interest you, and you will learn the most from. It's best if you buy a copy of the book to have forever. You can also try websites like Project Gutenberg to see if you can locate a free copy of the book.

Audiobooks:

If you're not the reading type of person, or you don't like eBooks, then audio books are probably for you. You can find audio books of most books out there. Once you find the book from the above step, look to see if you can find its audio book. That way, you can listen to the book while you work or in the car.

Music:

This one won't teach anything about your niche unless your niche is music, but it can help you to focus. Jazz or classical music can increase your intelligence as well as give you background ambiance when you're working. There are many places online to listen to this music for free. This is a good option to play while you are reading, or working on your niche.

Online Classes:

Many schools and universities are now posting free class content in the form of notes or podcasts. If you do a little research, it shouldn't be too hard to find information and classes based on your niche. There are also websites, like Coursera, that offer millions of classes online and offer a financial aid option that doesn't involve loans.

Educational Films:

Just like above, some universities are posting videos of their lectures online that you can access for free. Search through sites like YouTube to locate these types of videos.

E-mail Correspondence Course:

There are plenty of classes that you can have sent to you through your e-mail. You can receive a course on just about any subject, so you shouldn't have a problem finding something about your niche.

Before you can become an expert in your niche, you have to

learn as much as possible. Start using some of the above suggestions for expanding your intelligence and knowledge today. If you are invested in your niche, then researching and learning about it won't seem that hard, or like a chore.

Networking

Another great way to learn about your niche is to talk with others in your niche. A mentor is a great way to start. Of course, you can't just walk up to people on the street and start asking them random questions. There are right ways and wrong to go about this, and we're going to look at some of the appropriate ways.

Before you can network, you have to find people to network with. Of course, networking can be done at gatherings. You can choose to walk around and talk to random people at parties and get information that way, but it's helpful to have that one special person that you know you can turn to if you need help. Let's look at some ways to find a mentor.

- Figure out somebody that you would like to be.

Don't just look for people that are within the job you want to have, or have a service that you wish you had thought of. Look at people that are similar to you, that have skills and strengths similar to yours. If you don't, then you're going to end up frustrated. Take some time trying to find the right person. Make a list of several people before you choose just one.

- Study your person.

Follow their social media platforms. Study the people that are already friends with them. If you don't already know the person, see if they truly are the way they appear online. Get to know their weaknesses and strengths. Make sure that your expectations are realistic.

- Ask them.

Don't automatically ask them to be your mentor. That's a huge step with no build up, and especially for a first meeting.

Instead, ask them for a meeting in an informal setting, such as coffee. Try to keep it under an hour as well. Have some questions ready, but let the meeting flow generally. You probably won't ever feel like it's the right time to ask for a meeting, so just go for it.

- Evaluate them.

After that first meeting, do you feel like you would like to spend even more time with them? Were they encouraging, or did they tell you what should be done? Did they like to ask the questions or answer them? Did you feel better after the meeting? Were you able to make a connection? If you didn't feel good about it, then let this person go and look for somebody else. You don't have to go with your first choice or even your second choice. If you did feel good about it, then start planning your second meeting.

- The follow-up.

This isn't dating, so it's okay if you appear ambitious. It's important that the person knows that you are serious. The appropriate thing to do is immediately follow up and thank the person for their time. It's best to do this through e-mail or some other passive communication. This way you won't come off as overbearing and their time won't be wasted. It's also important to mention that you would like to meet up again. If the person replies, then start planning for the next meeting. It should all feel very relaxed and not forced.

- Allow it to grow organically.

The biggest mistake you can make is putting too much importance and too high of an expectation on finding a mentor. Everybody thinks you need to put a name to it, but all it is is a relationship. It needs to be organic. It's healthier to allow it to grow the same as any other relationship. It should be based on mutual trust and respect. If you force it, you will likely kill the relationship.

- Don't give up if you start feeling challenged.

Something that everybody is probably guilty of is, checking out when the going gets tough. It's going to get tough, things will test you, but you have to push through. Your mentor will call you out once in a while. How you react is crucial to how you grow. This is why you are seeking a mentor. You have to take the bad to get to the good.

- Lead if you have to.

There is no need to wait for your mentor to initiate. Persevere, and don't be afraid to ask your mentor for more, but you have to make sure you don't demand it. It shouldn't bother them when asking for more. It should make them feel honored. It shouldn't matter if you ask them to meet for lunch or coffee outside of the times you usually meet. If they are uncomfortable in being a friend, and being there for you, then they probably aren't going to be a good mentor.

- Ask for feedback.

Feedback is hard to receive, but it plays a useful purpose. As the relationship grows with your mentor, this is how you are going to grow. It will start out feeling weird to ask for feedback, but it will soon become normal. You will find that you need their words of advice.

- Commit to them.

You can't be helped in one summer. This is a full-time job, and mentoring takes work and time. For it to be real, you have to commit to the relationship you have built. No matter what is thrown at you, you are willing to make this work. You will soon begin to understand what it means to be a protégé.

Questions

To be able to find a mentor and learn things from them, you are going to have to know how to ask questions. This may seem like it should be simple, but it takes the right kind of questions to make things work. You may think their answers are bad, but maybe you aren't asking the right questions. Let's look at some ways to develop the best questions.

What is it that you are looking for?

Before you ask a question, you have to know what exactly you want to ask. Figure out if you are looking for cold, hard facts, or an opinion. Here are some questions to answer before you ask your question:

- Am I looking for a factual answer?
- Am I looking for an expert opinion?
- Am I looking for judgment?

Answer these, and you should be well on your way to asking a good question.

Avoid yes or no questions.

Yes or no questions only give you incomplete information. Ask open- ended questions instead. You will receive more insights with these types of questions. When you use words like "do you think," "are," "is," "should," or "would" will only give you yes or no. Instead use words like, "why", "how", "when", "where", "what", and "who". These will give you more information.

Follow up.

Chances are you aren't just looking for strict facts. When somebody answers a question, there are assumptions in the answer. Ask a follow up to their answer like, "Why is that?" or "Why do you say that?"

Allow there to be silence.

You have to accept the fact that there is going to be some silence. You ask questions, you sit and wait, they answer a question, and then you wait some more. Those pauses will give the person answering a chance to form their answer and will give you an opportunity to create a follow-up and process what they said.

Do not interrupt.

It's important that you never interrupt the person you are talking with. When you do, it tells them that you aren't interested in their opinion. It disrupts their thought process. Allow the person to answer your question completely before you say something. If they start to get long winded and they are straying from the subject; then nicely cut it. Say something like "Excuse me, let me make sure I understand what you're saying..." This will help to bring them back on topic.

If you use this information, you will be well on your way to asking the most useful questions. With good questions and a good mentor, you will learn the most information, and you get the most out of your meetings.

Social Media

Social media is the heartbeat of most successful businesses. When your goal is to become an expert in your niche, then you're going to have to prove it, and the best place to do so is through social media. Social media also gives you a great platform to sell any services and products that you may choose to make. This chapter will cover some of the benefits and uses of social media to become an authority in your niche.

Having niche-specific content will help you to bring in interested people, and will lead them to your websites. Writing niche-specific content to share on social media will do wonders for your business.

If you have too many social media platforms, you can make it difficult for your target customers to find your content. Most of the platforms out there are aimed towards miscellaneous information causing your message not to reach your audience. That's why you need to adopt these approaches:

1. Find platforms that are for your niche. Being active on platforms that cater to you niche will give you the best chance to attract potential customers. Some niche-based platforms include websites like Ravelry, Goodreads, and Cafemom. For example, Goodreads caters towards people who enjoy reading, whereas Cafemom caters towards moms. A little research is necessary to find the right platforms, and you will have to think outside of the norm, but you can find a platform for just about anything.

2. Make a small network. Sites like Instagram and Facebook gives you the ability to create subnetworks within their site. Facebook groups are one such example of these subnetworks. You could choose to join these groups and share your information and services

to people who are interested in it.

If you use the above strategies, you won't have to fuss with your content to find the right audience. These strategies put your content right in the hands of the people that are looking for it.

There are some social networks out there that are borderline niche platforms. These include LinkedIn, YouTube, and Pinterest. The way you share your content on LinkedIn is going to be very different than how you share things on YouTube. LinkedIn is more professional based. With YouTube, videos and animation are what people look at, on Pinterest, there need to be good-quality photographs to grab attention, and on LinkedIn, the text is what stands out.

One service is going to have to be marketed in different ways on each platform. This is important because the more information that you have to share, the more content you need to share. Keep in mind; not all information is going to fit into all platforms, especially borderline platforms. It's important to make sure that your content fits for a platform and if not, skip it.

After you have found your audience, you have to be able to engage them. Social media gives you an automatic way to engage them. Each social media platform has their unique selling point. With Facebook, you use announcements to engage. With Instagram and Pinterest, you use product pictures. DIY or informative videos are used to engage people on YouTube.

Social media also gives you a way to communicate with your audience. The purpose of niche-specific content is to engage people in conversations. That is where social media comes into play.

Now that you know the importance of social media, and what

it can do to elevate your authority in your niche, let's look at how you can decide if a platform is right for you.

Profitable Platform

The right network will depend on your niche, your goals, and your audience. 10% of businesses, in 2015, said that they marketed on social media for 16 to 20 hours each week. Instead of spending a bunch of time on Twitter and Facebook, find the best network to market on.

1. Figure out your target audience and make an online persona.

The first step in any marketing strategy is to figure out your audience's profile. This includes their challenges, fears, values, location, income, education, interests, gender, and age. After you have figured out your audience, you can start to create content that your audience would want to see.

2. Find the social networks where your audience frequents.

This is probably the hardest part, figuring out where to reach your audience. There are three ways that you can figure this out:

Use Buzzsumo and search a keyword that is related to your niche. It will give you the content that has been shared on social media platforms. This will help you to figure out which platforms are the most popular.

Create an audience that will benefit you in the long run. Facebook may be the easiest to build an audience, but it's going to cost you money. Also, if you spend time trying to market on the wrong site, you're going to end up wasting money. Finding a network where the audience can share your content, and where there isn't as much competition, you will be more successful at building an audience.

Look for overlaps between your social network and target audience. If your target audience is people in the 18 to 24 age group, then Snapchat and Instagram are going to be your best platforms. If you're looking to target professionals aged 24 to 44, then your best platform would be LinkedIn.

3. Check your competition and pick the one that aligns best with your goals.

If you see that your competition is getting more traffic than you, they have probably figured out how to crack the code on an individual platform. Some tools will allow you to understand how they are driving traffic, and then you can try to outdo them. Some tools that you can use to do this are Quintly and Ahrefs content explorer.

4. Grow your audience by using entertainment, education, and entertainment.

After you have gone through all the previous tips, you should have a good idea of where you can reach your target audience, and who they are. Now you have to give them the content they are looking for, and you need to do this in a way that will allow you to stand out. Four main elements lead to your content being shared; format, topic, content, and emotional. It's important to incorporate more than one of these elements to create a successful post.

5. Measure your results and keep working.

The only way you are going to become successful is if you do better than your competition. Keep track of how your marketing is going and continue to work at ways to make it better. Stand out from the crowd by doing things differently. Most platforms provide an area that shows how well your posts did. Use that to grow.

Social media will be your best friend while becoming an

authority in your niche. Once you figure out how to use it to your advantage, you will become a known expert in your field in no time.

Public Speaking

Most people, if asked, would say they despise public speaking. Of those people, only a few have a real, debilitating fear of public speaking. Being nervous about public speaking is understandable because you have the risk of messing up; which could cause you to be unforgettable for all the wrong reason.

With that being said, you can't completely avoid public speaking. You probably won't ever find public speaking fun, but you will learn how to deal with it. It's a necessary evil when it comes to becoming an expert in your niche.

Learning some public speaking skills will help to make you more comfortable, but if you hate public speaking, you're probably going to want some reasons to do so. Here are five reasons why you should learn more about public speaking.

1. It helps you to demonstrate knowledge. If you can articulate your information clearly, it's a great way to show people that you truly know what you are talking about.

2. It increases your knowledge. When you prepare a presentation, you will learn even more about your subject matter. The most important part of making a good presentation is knowing what you are talking about. It may seem simple, but it's true.

3. Creates and displays confidence. When you can talk to a large group of people, your confidence will increase. It can also help your standing with other people within your workplace or your competitors.

4. It will differentiate you. Public speaking isn't something that everybody is good at, so if you can develop the skill, you will stand out amongst your peers.

5. It helps to avoid risks in your career. If nothing else makes you want to learn public speaking look at it this way, being somewhat competent at it versus not, isn't going to put you at any disadvantage. If somebody listens to the same presentation, by two different people, and one is constantly stumbling over their words, and the other's not, people are going to like the first guy better.

Now ask yourself if you think that developing your public speaking skill is important for your goals?

How well do you think your current skills are and do you think you could use them confidently?

Have you ever witnessed people that have made either a good or a bad impression with their public speaking?

If you answered yes to any of those questions, then you are probably going to want to improve your public speaking skills. It doesn't have to be hard to learn; it only takes a few simple steps to improve your confidence and abilities.

First, you have to get comfortable with the thoughts of public speaking.

1. Change your outlook. Negative feelings towards public speaking will hinder your public speaking abilities. You have to switch the negative thoughts to positive thoughts. Pump yourself up before a speech. Tell yourself you can do this, or "I've got this." Thinking about how much you don't want to do the speech beforehand won't serve any purpose at all.

2. Become comfortable with the sound of silence. People use filler words like "um" and "uh" because they don't like hearing the silence during a pause. Having that silence is okay. The audience would rather hear silence while you gather your thoughts than hearing random noises.

After you have learned how to calm yourself for your speech, you're ready to prepare yourself.

1. Appropriately plan. Take time to put everything together for your speech. That way, when it's time to give it, everything will flow naturally, and it will feel normal. View it as if you were in a play. If you don't learn what you are supposed to say then you won't be able to engage your audience. The more you know your information, the more comfortable you will feel.

2. Record yourself practicing the speech. Practice your speech in front of a camera and then watch it back. Take note of the way you act, move, and speak. Change things up that you think are necessary.

3. Breathe, smile, and drink water. Breathing will help you stay focused and calm. Smiling helps to make you feel happy. Water will keep you energized and hydrated.

4. Rest and dress well. Get a full night's sleep before your speech. You will wake up feeling energized and ready for your speech. Make sure you dress well too. If you dress nicely, you will feel more comfortable.

The last thing you have to do is perform your speech.

1. Warm yourself up. Before you give your speech, do some stretches and vocal warm-ups.

2. Introduce yourself. Before you dive into your statement, introduce yourself to the group. Do this even if you are speaking in front of people that you know.

3. Begin by stating your thesis. Let your audience know what you are going to cover and briefly say the different parts of your speech.

4. Make eye contact, and keep good body language. Make a point of looking people in the eye when you speak. Make sure you also use hand and facial expressions.

5. Articulate. Your diction is an important part of a good speech. If the audience doesn't understand the things that you are saying, then they will end up tuning out of your speech.

6. Have energy. Your audience as an energy and you have energy. The audience will be able to sense if you are nervous. Also, don't follow the audience's energy, you should lead their energy.

7. Check your outline. Refer to the outline you made so that you don't get lost in your speech. The practicing you did should have prepared you fairly well, but that doesn't mean you should go at it without a cheat sheet. A glance at the outline now and then to make sure that you're staying on topic.

8. Have fun. A good public speaker will have fun with their speech. Feel proud of what you have accomplished, and excited about you're teaching your audience.

Now you shouldn't have any problems giving speeches on your niche. In fact, you should be so confident of your research and skills, you come off as an expert in your field.

YouTube

We talked earlier about the importance of social media, one of the platforms being YouTube. YouTube can be very helpful when you want to become an expert in your niche. Not only does it play a part in your learning process, but once you have information that you want to share with people, it gives you a great place to do so.

Having a YouTube channel puts you and your niche in front of a huge viewing audience. Around 800 million people around the world watch videos on YouTube each month, a lot of them using it to learn something new and how to make things.

If you can reach just a portion of that viewing audience with your personal, niche-based YouTube channel, the effort that it takes to make a video will pay off. YouTube is a great way to attract customers to a website, and for you to share information with other people.

Making a YouTube channel may not be the best choice for everybody, but chances are, it is. If you have any doubts about making a YouTube channel, here are ten questions to help you figure out how to make the best channel:

1. What is it that you want to achieve with a channel?

Figure out a specific goal before you begin uploading videos. When you have a clear vision of what you hope to achieve with your videos, then you will be able to make the most appropriate videos. For example, are looking to showcase a product, engage customers, drive sales, or to tell your story? You can also use your channel to answer questions that your customers may have.

2. Do you need to have multiple channels?

If your niche involves several, distinct areas, then it might be in your best interest to have different channels. This may be a bit harder to figure out, and depending on what your niche is, you probably won't need multiples. If your niche ends up becoming a company with several different products, then multiple channels are the way to go.

3. How should I change the background for my channel?

If you already have a website for your niche, mirror the look of your website on your YouTube channel. If you don't, then make your YouTube channel reflect your niche and what you are trying to teach or sell. With your channel, you can change the color of your background and upload background images.

4. Should you make commercials for your services and products?

People watch videos on YouTube for information, education, and entertainment, not for commercials. It's best to make informative and helpful videos that will enhance your image and not come off as promotional. For example, if your niche is cooking, post cooking tutorials with links to your products instead of trying to sell your cooking supplies or ingredients.

5. How do you properly tag and describe your videos?

Descriptions need to be concise; it should just be a couple of sentences. If you have a website, link to it within the first sentence or two. This encourages visits. It's also helpful to have keyword search terms within the description. If your video is a behind-the-scenes video of how you make German chocolate cake, then add tags such as "cake," "German chocolate," "baking," "frosting," and "gourmet." With tags like that, cake lovers can find you easily through internet searches and on YouTube.

6. How should you have your content organized?

Instead of having your videos in one long list, group them based on theme or topic. Viewers will be able to locate specific videos quickly and won't get bored trying to scroll through all of them.

7. Do you need to produce your own, and how often do you need to post?

Shooting your own or hiring a company to do it for you depends on how much money and time you are willing to invest. If you don't have the money to hire someone, shoot your own with your smartphone or an HD camera. After a while, the more money you make and the bigger budget you have, you can start to invest in better equipment or a studio. Post new videos as often as you can. If you can post a new and interesting video each week, then your audience will automatically start coming to you, and you will develop a loyal following.

8. Should you enable comments?

When you allow people to comment on your videos, you are encouraging them to talk and share their experiences with your services. It also gives a good place to find some feedback. You still have the ability to delete any comments that you don't want to have on your videos. If you're worried about comments, there is an option that allows you to approve the comment before it's posted.

9. How should you promote?

When you upload a new video, you should share a link to it on all of the social media platforms that you use for your niche. You can also embed the video on your website. You can also use sites like Google Adwords to help drive traffic to your videos.

10. How can you tell if your channel is successful?

With YouTube, you have access to all of your viewership analytics right at your fingertips. You will see how many people have viewed your videos, how often, and how they found them. You will also find how many subscribers you currently have, likes, dislikes, shares, and comments.

Using these questions, and the knowledge you have in your niche, you can grow an audience in no time. It may seem like a lot of work to you at first, but in the end, you will see all of it pay off.

Blogs and Podcasts

You can find blogs and podcasts on just about any subject nowadays, which means one of two things; either people love making them, or they are helpful in spreading the word. It's probably both of those things, but they can help you to stamp your place in history for your niche. Not only can you share information with people through these mediums, but they also can help if you develop a business around your niche.

Back in the olden days, which is 5 to 10 years ago in the age of the internet, a common question people were asked was if they were going to make a website for their business. Now that websites are a prerequisite for businesses, the question is, "Are you going to have a blog?" They become increasingly important as your niche-based company grows, and you look to find more customers.

Blogging does require the ability to create and write, as well as sharing information. If you don't have such abilities, you can hire people to help with your posts.

First, let's look at how blogs can help with your niche.

1.   They drive traffic to your niche-based website.

There are three main ways that people can find your website. One, they happen to type your name in a search engine, but chances are, that's an audience you already had. Second, you could use an e-mail list and blast them with e-mails and hope they click on a link. You shouldn't do that by the way; it's illegal. Third, you could buy ads to drive traffic, but once you run out of money, the traffic stops.

When you blog, it allows you to take up space on your website. With each new post you write, there is another page indexed on your site. This means that there is another chance that you will pop up on somebody's search engine when they are looking for information on something.

It also helps you get discovered on various social media sites, which we already know is very helpful. Each time you write a post, share it on your social media platforms. It also keeps up your presence on social media as well.

2. They are a low-cost marketing option.

The only things you have to pay for are a hosting service and a domain name. Those two things are more than enough to get you started with a successful blog.

3. It turns traffic into new leads.

I would safely assume that your niche is going to become your business. The whole point of this is to help you become an expert in that field, and in turn, you learn how to use that knowledge to turn a profit. If I'm wrong, then skip past this one. For those out there wanting to make this a business, then you're going to want to listen.

Blogs bring people to your site, but when they get to your site, they should see a call-to-action link offering a gift. They click on the call-to-action and type in their information. You get their e-mail address and name, and they receive whatever gift you were offering. You have a new lead, and they have something free that they want. Everybody wins.

Now you have a bigger audience to share your expertise with. Keep in mind that not every person that reads your blog will click that button, but the ones who do, are probably the audience that you are looking for.

4. Blogs establish authority.

The best kind of blogs will answer questions that people have. If you are always posting new blogs with content that your target audience finds helpful, it'll establish you as an expert to them. Think about how amazing it would feel to know that you were able to explain things for somebody with one of your blogs.

It may not be something that you can measure, like traffic or leads, but it is a powerful tool. If you can prove to be more of an authority in your niche than your competitors, then you will surpass them.

5. It gives you long-term results.

Wouldn't it be amazing if you could drive traffic to your site while you were on vacation in Hawaii, at the gym, or sleeping? You can. Blogs do that through search engines.

Look at it this way. You spend an hour writing and publishing a new blog. The next day, your blog gets 200 views and 20 leads. Then the next day you end up getting 100 more views and ten more leads. After a few days, the fanfare around your new post dies down, and you end up with 300 views and 30 new leads.

Your post isn't finished. During this time and after, it is ranking in search engines. This means for days, weeks, months, and even years after, you will continue to see traffic and leads coming from that blog post. The great thing is that traffic from a blog post grows over time, and it does so no matter what you are doing.

Hopefully, this shows how beneficial blogging can be to your niche and subsequent business. It may not show immediate results, as some things, but it has a long-term factor that other platforms can't beat.

There are some secondary benefits to blogging, but they are smaller and kind of stray from the bigger picture. For example, you can use your blog to test something out before you invest any money in the creation of the product.

Podcasts

Podcasts, if you don't know, are sort of like an audio blog. It gives your audience the information they want when, where, and how they want it. They are downloaded audio files that people can listen to anywhere they want. People, who subscribe, will receive the new podcasts as soon as you publish a new one.

Podcasts are being added to websites and blogs more often now. Business uses them for training and communication purposes. They are also extremely convenient.

Just like with a blog, the content is the important part of podcasts. Nobody is going to want to listen to somebody drone on about something that they don't find the least bit interesting. You don't want to sound preachy or deliver a monotonous presentation.

You have to create the content with your listening audience in mind. This includes their interests and their listening habits. A person has less patience for recorded content than they do for live content.

You have to think like a radio producer. They know that their listeners can switch the station any time that they want to. That's why they focus on entertainment value. When somebody listens to your podcasts, they will typically be alone and can switch it off as soon as they stop feeling informed, entertained, or fulfilled. Here are some ways that you can make sure nobody turns off your content:

Give them valuable information. This value could be in the form of entertainment, motivation, inspiration, information, and education. Don't just make your podcasts sound like infomercials; nobody likes listening to those.

Conversations work. Think about having other people on your podcast. This means you can have people on that you interview or that interview you. You can also get a lot of people together and have a panel discussion. One-person podcasts aren't exactly dynamic, and dynamic podcasts sell.

Remember: promote, promote, promote. Make sure to end your podcasts by encouraging people to subscribe and sign-up. Let them know that they will receive a regular update, and they will know as soon as a new podcast has been published.

Podcasting gives you another way to market to your target audience, and show that you are an authority in your niche. Remember, you can also post on social media every time you publish a new podcast.

Teaching Others

If you practice any of the past things discussed in the previous chapters, then you will likely be teaching others about your niche. You may not have started this with teaching in mind, but if you are looking to become an expert in your field, then teaching will help you do so.

At this point in your journey, you have probably become, somewhat, of an expert in your niche. You've developed some skills, experience, and knowledge that make you an authority on the subject. What should you be doing with the knowledge? Sure, you may have a blog or podcast, and maybe several social media networks or a YouTube channel, but are still holding your information like a squirrel hordes nuts? You may just be using your expertise to further yourself, and not considering how you could help others.

You are probably very tempted to keep all that information you have to yourself, but it's a powerful gift that you should share with others. You may have earned it, but if you don't share it, then how will others know you are an expert.

When you share your knowledge, you can help others in their professional career, as well as your own. Here's how it helps:

1. It contributes to engrain the information that you possess.

When you share your knowledge, you deepen your knowledge. If you don't ever use the information in some way, then you will likely forget it.

2. It helps to expand the things that you know.

When you share your knowledge, you invite new conversations. If you are willing to listen and learn from others, then you may discover something new.

3. It will establish your reputation as an expert.

If your goal is to be an expert and leader in your niche, then you have to be able to stand out and become vocal about the things you can offer. You can tell people all day long that you're an expert, but that doesn't mean anything. Give them a taste of what you know, and show them that you're an expert.

4. It will increase your value.

When your knowledge can help your whole team, or niche, you will become more valuable. You will be worth more when you can show that you are an expert, and this will translate to rewards and dollars.

Now, you may be thinking that you don't want to come off as arrogant. If this is your belief, then you need to change your perspective. Sharing your knowledge isn't something you do out of arrogance. You are of service to others. It isn't about you, but them. Here are some ways that you can share your expertise.

1. Become a mentor.

There are plenty of young people out there looking for guidance, just like you were at one time. When you discover a newbie that has lots of potential but could use some support, take them under your wing and guide them. Share information with them that you have learned. While doing so, be sure to keep yourself open to learning things from them. When it's a healthy relationship, you both will reap benefits.

2. Write.

Writing is a great way to reach out to others. You could write an article for some niche-based publication. You can also start a blog. It's empowering to put your thoughts about something out there. The connections you can make with people through your writing are life changing. Plus, once you become published, no matter if it's online or in print, you are automatically given a level of authority. It may seem weird to hear, but writers are automatically seen as experts, even if they don't truly know what they're talking about.

3. Train people.

Put yourself out there, and volunteer to present information on a topic at meetings or conferences within your niche. If you have developed a big following or business, host a learn and lunch event. Present everything you know about a topic in a confident manner that enlightens and engages the audience. Don't talk down to the people; you should tap into the wisdom of the people listening to you. Make sure to open the conversation up so that the guests can share their knowledge. Never assume that you are the only person that has something to say on a topic. This will also help you boost your skills in public speaking, and will position you as an expert.

4. Become a resource.

If you happen to stumble upon a helpful article, a new piece of information, or a better way to do something, don't just keep the info for yourself. Chances are, you have something helpful that you can share with others. You don't have to wait for somebody to ask you to help them with something, or for a formal training session. Instead, when you find something precious, send an e-mail to your audience, or write a post. Think about how you would feel if somebody did the same for you. It's a nice gesture, and people will appreciate you for it.

5. Become a leader.

If you are asked to be a part of a group, and you know that you have a beneficial expertise, don't be afraid to take the reins on the project. There are a lot of knowledgeable people out there that won't take the lead because they are afraid to, or, unfortunately, just don't care. Don't be one of those. Share your knowledge and take the lead.

It's worse to make people have to beg for your help. It will be more appreciated if you volunteer to give the information out freely. Step up and be a leader. Your goal is to become an expert; then you need to prove you are an expert.

Products and Services

Services and products are how businesses and niches survive. They aren't typically something that is just optional; they are crucial to your growth. But setting out to develop one can seem daunting and risky. You have to make sure you organize and plan. Here, I'm going to cover how to know when it's right to develop a new service and how to do so.

Lifecycle

There are five main stages in a service or products lifecycle:

Development – this is when your service or product is just an idea. This is where you invest your time in development and research.

Introduction – this is where you launch the service or product. You are investing your time in marketing.

Growth – this when the service or product is beginning to establish itself. You're making a profit, sales are growing, and you don't have as many competitors. This is when you start looking at reducing the cost of delivery.

Maturity – this is where sales growth slows or stops. You've reduced marketing and production costs, but your competition has caused your prices to reduce as well. This is when you start to think of a new product.

Decline – there are now new services or products on the market. Your sales and profit margins have declined. Marketing isn't going to help and definitely won't be cost-effective.

Knowing where your service or products are in their lifecycle is extremely important to your success. Having done enough research is also important so that you make sure you are doing the best you can to market against your competitors.

Development

To help you minimize risk and to make sure that you consider all of these factors when you are developing a service or a product:

- Will the product meet the specifications that the customer is looking for? Look at its benefits, ease of use, and design.

- Is the service or product technologically feasible? Can you meet the requirements to manufacture and design the item?

- Do you know exactly what you want to achieve with the service or product? Will it meet what you have planned out and does it work with the strengths of your business?

The clearer you are about what you want, the better off you will be.

Matching Market Needs

Your services or products have to benefit your customers, and you have to figure out what those needs are. Focus groups and surveys can help you to identify these things. You have to also take into consideration the needs of people that aren't your most important customers.

For example, if you were developing a new fitness product, you have to think about how stores would stock your item, as well as how it can help the fitness community. If you are making something marketed towards children, you have to think about what parents think as well.

You also have to do all of this in a way that makes you stand out from your competition. It needs to have a unique selling point. Some property or feature that stands out. Before you continue, make sure you know how to answer the following:

- How are your customer's needs currently being met?

- Why would people pick your product over somebody else's, now and in the future?

- What are the risks that you are okay with taking when you launch the service or product?

Pricing

Another extremely important part of the development process is figuring out how you are going to price your product. The moment you decide you are going to move an idea forward, you need to figure out pricing because it will tell you how much money you can invest.

Take these factors into consideration:

- The value or benefit it will have to customers over your competitions. Will customers be willing to pay your price?

- Are you first on the market? Are you following trends and is your service revolutionary?

- Look at the selling channels you plan on using.

- How quickly you want to establish your service.

- How you expect its lifecycle to go.

- If you will be able to cover your costs.

Development Process

Here are the different stages of your development process:

- Idea generation – when you come up with new ideas.

- Idea distillation – when you get rid of ideas that aren't

worth the risk.

- Concept definition – when you look at market potential and feasibility. This is where you look at the design.

- Strategic analysis – when you make sure this fits into your plans.

- Concept development – when you make a prototype or pilot.

- Testing and finalizing – when you make sure that you can fix a product or service depending on the feedback you get. This is where you figure out your best timeline for piloting your new service.

- Product launch – before you can launch you have to figure out how you will support, promote, and sell your service or product. This is essential to the success of the product.

Investment

You have to make sure you plan appropriately to make sure you make money, and you don't lose money.

You need to consider the following:

- Factor in any future investments you may have into your plan.

- Plan where you will direct these investments.

- Justify the costs of each project

- Manage all of your costs.

Before you make any decisions, make sure you consider if you will gain from the service or product. A great way to minimize risks is to look at investments at the end of each phase in your development process. You should:

- Look at possible development costs before you begin.

- Monitor your expenses throughout the whole process.

- Practice looking at costs at the end of each phase.

Now that you know the best way to approach developing a service or product, you can begin looking at ways to profit from your niche. This is a great way to share your knowledge and expertise with people that are interested.

Improve Yourself

At this point, you have become an expert in your niche, and you may be thinking that there is nothing left to do, but you're wrong. Even if you think you know all there is to know about your niche, there's more. There is always more to learn about everything. Things change all the time. New information becomes available, and more efficient ways to do things becomes known. An important part of being an expert is making sure that you stay an expert, and one sure-fire way of doing that is by continuing to learn about your niche.

Your learning doesn't have to end. Your learning should be a lifelong goal and experience. Continuing to learn, and staying an expert, can easily be done in these ten simple ways:

1. Be curious, always.

Curiosity is one of the best ways to continue learning no matter what stage of life or learning you're in. When you are curious, you long to learn. You start to look for ways to find out more.

2. Start a new hobby.

There are lots of hobbies out there that you can learn. These hobbies are not only fun, but they teach you things as well. You can probably find a new hobby within your niche as well, which will teach you something that you never knew.

3. Add non-fiction to your library.

Most people enjoy reading fiction, and it's probably what takes up the majority of their bookshelf, but non-fiction will give you new experiences and teach you things. These books will help you to learn more about your niche and other things in life, which can open your sights to new things you could do.

4. Watch news-ish shows, and listen to podcasts.

Even if you don't enjoy watching the regular news, you can learn relevant information in a way that's not so dry. You can listen to podcasts, or you can watch shows like "The Daily Show" so that you can find out about the news in a way that's entertaining.

5. Go to lectures and events.

Going to events and lectures about your niche is a great and fun way to learn more. These types of events are also a great way to meet potential customers and other people within your niche.

6. Listen to what others have to say.

Talk to others about their experiences and life. Take in what they have to say. You can learn a lot about things through stories. You can also learn from any mistakes that they have made so that you don't make them as well. You should also still have a relationship with your mentor, so don't forget to talk to them.

7. Utilize all the media you have access to.

Use the internet and social media. You have millions of places to learn more about your niche at your fingertips. There is never a time when you can't look up things and look for new discoveries. It's probably one of the easiest ways to learn things, and it's free.

8. Have an open mind.

You can't become educated, or an expert, if you keep a closed mind. It's important to have an open mind and look at things in a different way. So that when you do come up with an opinion, you will have done so after looking at all the possible solutions.

9. Take a class.

Most community colleges offer classes that anybody can take without having to join a program or degree. These typically don't cost that much. If you are looking to learn something specific and you find a class on the subject, and then go for it.

10. Travel.

You may know everything there is to know about your niche in your home state or country, but other states and countries may have different views. Traveling the world is a great way to expand your horizons and to make sure that you know as much as possible. You may also have customers in other countries, so it's helpful to get a close look at what their world is like so that you make sure that you are offering them the best services and products possible.

If you practice these ten things, you will ensure that you stay an expert in your field. Now, I know that some of you may be thinking, "But I don't have the time for this." While this could be partly true, you should still be able to find ways to learn new things. I know you've probably got a lot going on, but there are five easy ways to ensure that you continue learning:

1. Prioritize your time. If your schedule is always busy, start scheduling learning time into your calendar. Set aside some time each day or week where you do something that will help you learn new things. You could simply read a book or take a class.

2. Make the most out of your meetings. Meetings can be a boring must in the business world, but if you use them properly, they can be a great way to learn new things. After all, you are meeting with another expert in your field. They may have stumble across something new, so make sure you pay attention, and you just might learn something.

3. Join a group. There are plenty of groups out there that you can join, and you can make sure they're niche-based as well. Chances are, you are probably already a part of some groups. This can be a good way to find out new information that you haven't become aware of yet.

4. Read everything you can. I can't stress the importance of books enough. I've talked about them several times already, but they really should be your best friend. Schedule reading time, or at least read for a few minutes before you go to bed. Don't just read books that are about your niche, broaden your horizons a little.

5. Teach a class. This works with the chapter on teaching, when you teach people things, you will likely learn more yourself. When you have to take the time to research everything about what you are teaching, you're sure to stumble across new information that you weren't aware of.

Practice all of the above, and you will stay at the head of the game. You should never fall behind in your niche, and you will always be the go-to person when somebody is looking for information.

Conclusion

Thank for making it through to the end of *Expert Enough.* Let's hope it was informative and able to provide you with all of the tools you need to achieve your goals of becoming an expert.

The next step is to figure out your niche. Start implementing the things you have learned to begin building your expertise in a field that you love. You will soon find that people come to you for advice, and trust you to have the correct information. You may even have somebody come to you looking for you to be their mentor.

Finally, if you found this book useful in any way, a review on Amazon is always appreciated!